Sugar Cube

A Collection of Poems

Sihem Hammouda

@2024 AEEH PRESS IN

Middle East Manager and Editor: Ahmed M. Shalaby

Cover Design: Kareem Metwalee & Mahmoud Assad

This Collection contains prose poems with intellectual depth generated from realistic and imaginary paradoxes that carry sarcasm at times and mild sadness at other times. It deals with childhood memories, children's games, the doll's matchmaker, talking about the refugees, the practices of politicians, and so on. The poetess takes you to her magical world in a calm, delicate language, with inspiration and amazing mastery.

AEEH PRESS INC

As a Tunisian translator and writer, she works in the field of education, especially teaching English language. In 2016, a collection of short stories entitled "The Stranger" was published for her. Moreover, a collection of poetry in English titled "Arabian Roses' Whispers" was published by the French house, Edilivre in 2016, in addition to the collection of short stories "The Buttons Thief" issued by Washma House for Publishing and Distribution in 2022.

She is still publishing in many paper and electronic newspapers and magazines, such as Intelligentsia for Culture and Free Thought, Egyptian Merit Magazine, Al Sharq Magazine (Iraq), Algerian Cultural Magazine, a Romanian magazine dealing with translation called "Our Poetry Archive, "Letters of Poetry Magazine, Today's Opinion, Omani Vision Newspaper, Universal Poetry, Donia Al Watan, and Arab Lit Quarterly.

Among the literary works she has translated, the collection of poems "The Revelation of Aphrodite" by the Algerian poet Soumaya Mubarak was published in 2017 by Dar Maher for publishing and distribution. She has also translated the collection of poems "My Love and the Homeland" by the Syrian poet Ahmed Turkmani, published by Al-Rehab Modern Institution for Printing, Publishing and Distribution. In addition, she has translated the novel "The Truth" by the Lebanese writer Muhammad Iqbal Harb, published by Aeeh Press for publishing and translation in California. She also translated the short stories "Different Tastes" collection by the Tunisian writer Lamia Boukil, published by Aeeh Press for publishing and translation in California. Then, she has translated the collection of short stories "Outside the Domain of Erosion" by the Algerian writer and poetess Dr. Fadila Milhaq, published by Dar Al-Amir for publication, distribution, and translation. Finally, she has translated the novel "When Life Desires You" by the Algerian writer and poetess Dr. Fadila Milhaq, published by Dar Al-Ain for publishing in Egypt.

Dedication

To my mother, father, and brothers,
To everyone who taught me letters,
To my younger sister Sondos, who loves what I write.

Table Of Contents

The Beggar and Love

He gathered his longings and the remnants of his pride,
And then pillowed on a night
He wished it would never end.
In his dreams him visited
A pretty woman who danced with him,
And poems to him read.

Then, the moon and her anklet
Signed their insanity document.
When morning breathed,
And his breaths cooled,
He rose from his dance
And started to look in the midst of the throng of perfumes
For his sweetheart,
But fate slipped into his pocket
A hot loaf of bread,
And thus his love he forgot,
And hung on his life's coat rack
Another day with loneliness.

Love or War?

Her lips intoxicated by his farewell swayed,
And her arrows let out a sigh,
We were created for love!
The bow fidgeted with indifference,
Soon night fire will fade,
And he will wrap himself with the ceremonies
Of his departure,
We are created for war!

A day passed, then a night,
A spring and a winter to them paid a visit,
He turned his military helmet
Into a nest for pigeons,
And then pronounced his bow and arrows
A husband and a wife.

Hide and Seek

Do not worry, my dolly!
This is not a gunshot,
This is uncle Hassan
Trying his old musket,
For tomorrow is his daughter Safia's wedding.
I will comb your gold tresses,
And dress you in a pink frock,
While I will wear
My mother's silver bangles.

One... two... three
I'm coming...

Look sweetie,
This is Jinan's hair ribbon,
She made it out of her mother's dress,
Do you remember Aunt Fikria?

She used to weave for us woolen socks.
To protect us against winter coldness,
Jinan told me that she in the sky lives,
That's why the winter here so cruel,
And neighborhood children wear
Only black socks.
One... two... three...
I'm coming...

look,
This is Salah Al-din's wooden sword,
You know Salah Al-din!
That boy who doesn't love eating lollipop,
They said that
Once a stranger gave him a piece of candy,
And then stole his sister's white tippet,
Two years passed,
A piece of candy in his pocket,
And a hungry sword in his right hand.

One... two...
The sun hid too,
We have to go home, sweetie,
I can hear an anklet's chime
Resembling my mother's anklet this time,
It must be the baker's wife distributing bread to houses,
Smile, my sweet,
We are going to eat hot bread this night,
One... two... three...
One... two... three...
I'm coming!

The Wife of an Arab Politician

You and your Cuban cigar looked
Like a white cloud
Teasing an iceberg,
And I and my red scarf looked
Like a music note
With which tune disputed.

My diamond watch reads nine,
Your evening appointment with your spoiled newspaper.
Sometimes I wonder,
Why you only read local news
In French
Or the truth looks
With a foreign pen less hideous,
And feelings look less fictitious.
You have to try the word "my sweetheart"
In Arabic
It is as sweet as sugar.

Thousand light years passed,
And I'm still looking among my grandmother's secret recipes
For a route to your heart.
Is there any news about her diamond anklet?
Did they find it?
Did you hear about the poor old woman
Who stole and then died of sadness
For hunger took her rosary away from her?

Forgive my ignorance;
I forgot that today
Is the celebration day
Of the heroism of politicians.

. . . .

A Tea Party for Scarecrows

Since when have you been here?
Since Man learned how to bake his bread.
You face is pale, dear;
You can rest on my shoulder your beautiful head...
All scarecrows that came before you used to tell me that.
Were any scarecrows here before me?
Hundreds of them!
That's wonderful, my sweetheart!
What about having a tea party
And inviting all scarecrows?
Do not call me sweetheart!
It is a time of barrenness and drought;
I don't understand
Why they make us
Guard dull fields?
Scarecrows were not created to understand or think.
Your dress is beautiful like your eye color,
Will you dance with me?
My grandma used to dance to the music of crows.
O poor spikes
Life fire is doused in you.
Hush! The night fell!
Do you feel scared of night when I'm beside you

My spoiled sweetheart?
Ah rain! Rain!
This is not rain patter, stupid

It's their drumbeats,
Whenever they lost a child in the field,
"The scarecrows ate him," they said.
These are the rituals of your death, honey.
So, are you going to let
A death-sentenced scarecrow
Have his last dance with you?

Hello, handsome!
Since when have you been here?
Since I encountered a scarecrow whose eye color
Resembles that of the sky.

The Moon's Moan

This night is so quiet,
I'm alone in the company of the moon
Counting our losses,
He is moving fast toward morning,
While I'm moving fast toward madness.
One evening his star fell down on the ground
While my sweetheart was crowned
A queen on another country other than mine
At the end of a winter,
And the worst of betrayals is that of homeland.
Longing seized me and the moon
And we don't know a cure for desertion or treason,
The sky doesn't rain,
Eyes don't weep,
Night mourns me and him,
No star can make him forget desertion
And no lips can ease my pain.
Ah!... Ah!...Ah!
"I think I heard the moon moaning last night,"
Said a lover kept awake by love.
"As if I saw a star waving to the sky
At the hill this morning,"
Said another lover.

A Crazy Poetess

My love lives in a poetry book
As poems' prisoner,
Poetry fears that if released,
It will drown in a sea
Of tears,
For its words were infatuated with his laughs
That they were weaving into moans
For poets.
My poems were torn asunder by my anger,
And my jealousy burned all my words,
For my love is my prisoner.

A Seventy-Year-Old Love

Why do you face away from me, my sweet?
What stupid thing did this old man do in my absence?
Have pity on me,
For without you I'm not good at arranging my steps.

Sweetheart...sweetheart!

I the silverware you like dusted,
And brought a frame for the photo of our grandchild,
Did you fix the hole in my woolen socks,
Darling?
Winter is approaching,
And this old man cannot stand cold evening.
Say something!
Oh, my God
What stupid thing did this old man do in the presence of my
beloved!?

What about traveling to Paris?
I know how much you love French perfumes,
Or India's colors to paint your velvet muffler?
It turned seventy years old like me!
Get closer,
I will tell you a secret darling,
My teeth fell out this morning,
It is the first tooth that witnesses our eternal love

Her eyes widened,
She smiled,
And he smiled.
She said,
My tooth fell out too
This morning
When I was roses planting.

My Beloved and the Rain

He happened to turn around,
And see her teasing the drunk ground,

With her bare toes like a spoiled child.

She turned to him, and his oriental eyes

Embraced hers as

An expatriate embracing an old letter

From his torn homeland.

"Do you love her?" she asked.

"Who?" he said.

"The rain," she answered.

"Yes I do."

He smiled.

"Who do you love more, me or her?"
She asked.

He smiled affectionately at her,

"Are you jealous of the rain?"
He asked.

"The rain is a woman, isn't she?"
She said.

"Yes she is. For this reason I love her."

Her dormant revolt was ignited

By a rain drop that broke gracefully along his lips,

And then traveled secretly to his covert cities.

She averted her dewy eyes,

And black pearls fell down

Her burning soft cheeks.

He approached her laughing,
"Woe to me!"
He said,
"Do you feel jealous of the rain?"

Ah, I wish!

I wish my home was a book,

I would live in a fairy tale,

And live happily ever after.

I would conquer wonderland

In children's stories

And then surrender it to orphans.

I would steal a magic wand,

To rekindle old women's smiles,

Be a knight,

And reign a land

Wherein bread is for all

And water is dulcet

And untarnished like a maiden's soul.

Death

His dreams are older
Than his shoes,
And his life is an aged tree
Leaning against time.
He walked through life path
Looking for a soul that resembles him
Or perhaps may remind him of his olden soul,
But every soul he met,
Is an olden one
Looking for a soul that resembles it or reminds it About what it was
like.
And there behind
The long night
Death crouches
On time
Craving dreamy souls.

To My Old House

A moan of an old swing,
A wounded door creak,
And shy whispers, the music accompanying
That of the feet of the displaced.
Ah, homeland!
Was the way toward you east?
Or west?
Or south?
Or north?
For crows ate my bread crumbs,
How could I find my way home?
They displaced jasmine trees,
The immigrants' compass.
How would my homeland find me?
They maimed me.
This sells bonds of death,
And that changed the attire of homeland.
Ah, my homeland!
I could not recognize me.

The Prisoners and the Sky

The prisoner ran away!
The jailor cried out.
The prisoners laughed
As high as the sky
Whose color they forgot.

My grandpa used to
Swear by my grandma's eyes
Whenever they accused him of a robbery.
Blue?
The prisoners cheered.
I have never known
For my grandma has one grey eye,
And another blue.

The prisoner was caught!
The jailor cried out.
The prisoners danced
And they stretched their necks
To see the sky messenger.
O prisoner,
Tell us about its color,
For confusion manipulated us
And depleted our patience.
The prisoner smiled.
What is its color?

I walked under it for days.
What is its color?
And I felt the warmth of its soul
Touching my soul.
What is its color?
O clowns!
Why does a blind like me
Need to know the color of the sky?

Eureka, Eureka

Eureka, Eureka,
Cried the young inexperienced crow,
And his cries tore the long night blanket.
Far away an old crow,
As old as dreams was watching him.
He spreads his tired wings,
And to the firmament, he lifted his eyes,
The stars sprinkle but they are not gold.
He closed his eyes and intently listened
To salt beads' chimes,
The blue ocean shines but it's not gold,
If you spend your journey
Looking down at the ground
Looking for gold,
You will never savor
The sweetness of soaring high.

Eureka, Eureka.

A Love Music Note

Hello, O piano.
Are you fine?
Your fingertips are cold.
Ah...
How much I envy you friend!
All women are in love with you
Both young and old.
Do you know that a long time passed,
So long like the path of the displaced,
Since a beautiful girl has written to me a love letter,
And dyed her hair for me.
She was a Jewish girl,
Or perhaps an Arab,
Forgive me for I can't remember very well
Where my sweetheart comes from,
For women become alike
When they fall in love.
What was her name?
What was her name?
Eva!
No, that was the sweetheart's name of our Sheikh Hitler.
Do you know that Hitler loved a Jewish girl?
She burned his heart, so he burned Jewish children's dolls,
Perhaps wars are a revenge on love.
O piano, tell me your secret!
My fingers are rough,
My body is shabby,

And my rifle overburdens me.
They gave us hungry rifles
That are never satiated,
A perfume that does not hide
Blood scent lingering on our dreams,
And then sent us to spread peace.
Can I have a love music note,
O friend?
I feel hungry
For a long time passed,
So long…
Since I have tasted
Music other than that played by rifles.

The Cloud and the Desert

I'm exhausted like a cloud
That the wind led toward the desert,
"Be a life ambassador here!"
A call from heaven ordained me,
Impart roses to thorns!
And with life fill land cups
Till drunkenness, till deathlessness.
That cloud said to the desert,
"Give me your thorns
And I will give you flowers
And turn your flaming breaths into coldness."
But the desert was indifferent,
For the desert without its thorns and blaze
Is but a shepherd without a flute,
A pen without ink,
And a prayer without submissiveness.
The cloud goes away...
And the desert remains a desert.